How Toys Spin

Helen Whittaker

MACMILLAN LIBRARY

First published in 2011 by
MACMILLAN EDUCATION AUSTRALIA PTY LTD
15–19 Claremont Street, South Yarra 3141

Visit our website at www.macmillan.com.au or go directly to www.macmillanlibrary.com.au

Associated companies and representatives throughout the world.

National Library of Australia Cataloguing-in-Publication data

Whittaker, Helen.
   How toys spin / Helen Whittaker.
   ISBN: 978 1 4202 8408 9 (hbk.).
   Whittaker, Helen. MYL toys and forces.
   Includes index.
   For primary school age.
   Rotational motion – Juvenile literature. Toys – Juvenile literature.
530.113

Publisher: Carmel Heron
Commissioning Editor: Niki Horin
Managing Editor: Vanessa Lanaway
Editors: Emma de Smit and Tim Clarke
Proofreader: Helena Newton
Designer: Kerri Wilson
Page layout: Romy Pearse
Photo researcher: Wendy Duncan (management: Debbie Gallagher)
Illustrator: Ned Culic (Colourist: Natalie Stuart)
Production Controller: Vanessa Johnson

Printed in China

Acknowledgements
The publisher would like to thank Heidi Ruhnau, Head of Science at Oxley College, Victoria, for her assistance in reviewing
manuscripts.

The author and publisher are grateful to the following for permission to reproduce copyright material:

Front cover photograph: Boy with yo-yo © MEA Images/Image Source.

Photographs courtesy of: Corbis/Beau Lark, **5** (top), /Eyetrigger Pty Ltd, **4** (bottom left); Dreamstime/Cebas1, **5** (bottom),
/Terrence Meehan, **9** (centre), **16**; Fotolia/Blacqbook, **8** (left), **10**; iStockphoto/HiDesignGraphics, **18**, /maica, **8** (right), **12**,
/Mitshu, **9** (bottom); MEA Images/Image Source, **1**, **4** (bottom centre); photolibrary/Alamy/Aurora Photos, **4** (bottom right),
/Alamy/Graham Corney, **20**, /Ingram Publishing, **9** (top), **14**; Pixmac/Yuri Arcurs, **4** (top left); Shutterstock/cassiede alain,
4 (top right), /Michael William, **4** (top centre), /Ruta Saulyte-Laurinaviciene, **6**.

Contents

When a word is printed in **bold**, you can look up its meaning in the Glossary on page 31.

Toys and forces

Forces make toys work. Forces make toys start moving, change direction, speed up, slow down and stop moving. Forces also change the shape of some toys.

Bouncing toys

Floating toys

Flying toys

Rolling toys

Sliding toys

Spinning toys

None of these toys would work without forces.

What is a force?

A force is a push or a pull. When you push something it moves away from you. When you pull something it moves towards you.

When this girl applies a pushing force to the merry-go-round, it moves away from her.

When this boy applies a pulling force to the diabolo, it moves towards him.

How does a spinning toy work?

A spinning toy works when a pushing or pulling force makes it move. A spinning toy moves by turning round and round.

A pushing force makes this top start spinning.

Spinning toys move by spinning around a straight line called an **axis**. In most spinning toys, the axis passes through the middle of the toy.

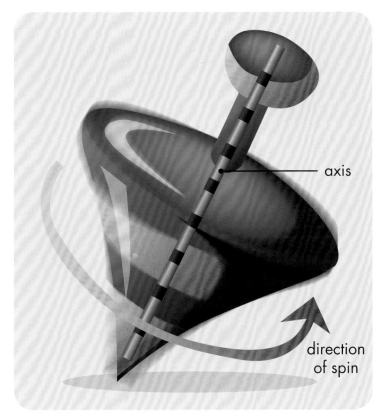

axis

direction of spin

This top spins around an axis, which passes through its middle.

How do forces make spinning toys work?

Different forces make spinning toys work. Pushes and pulls make the toys work in different ways. Forces can make spinning toys work in these ways.

Forces can make spinning toys start moving.

Forces can make spinning toys change direction.

Forces can make spinning toys speed up.

Forces can make spinning toys slow down.

Forces can make spinning toys stop moving.

What makes a spinning toy start moving?

When forces act on a spinning toy they can make it start moving. One force that can make a spinning toy start moving is a pushing force.

A yoyo starts moving when you apply a pushing force with your hand.

You can make a spinning toy start moving by pushing it. This applies a pushing force to the toy, which makes the toy start spinning.

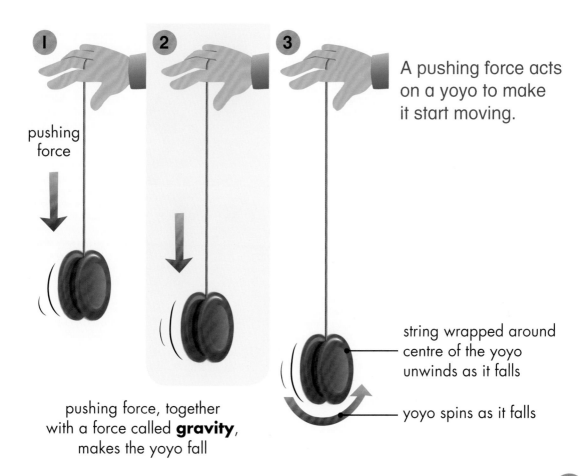

1

pushing force

pushing force, together with a force called **gravity**, makes the yoyo fall

2

3

A pushing force acts on a yoyo to make it start moving.

string wrapped around centre of the yoyo unwinds as it falls

yoyo spins as it falls

What makes a spinning toy change direction?

When forces act on a spinning toy they can make it change direction. One force that can do this is the pushing force created by moving air.

The pushing force created by moving air can make a windmill change direction.

Some spinning toys are designed to spin when the air around them moves. The pushing force created by moving air can make this kind of toy change direction.

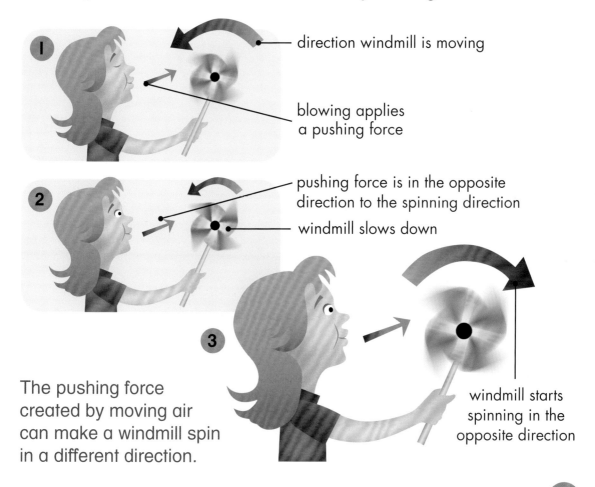

direction windmill is moving

blowing applies a pushing force

pushing force is in the opposite direction to the spinning direction

windmill slows down

The pushing force created by moving air can make a windmill spin in a different direction.

windmill starts spinning in the opposite direction

What makes a spinning toy speed up?

When forces act on a moving spinning toy they can make it speed up. One force that can make a spinning toy speed up is a pushing force.

A pushing force from a racquet can make a totem tennis ball speed up.

You can make a moving spinning toy speed up by applying a large pushing force to it. When the pushing force acts on the toy, the toy spins faster.

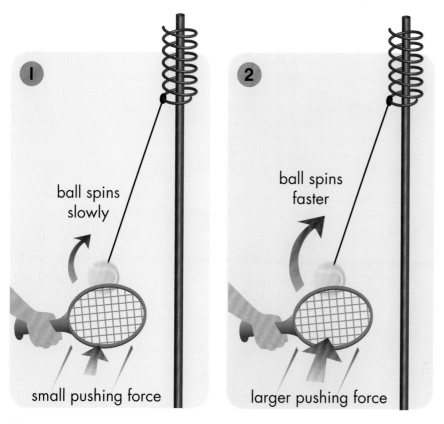

Hitting the moving ball harder gives it a larger pushing force, so it spins faster.

What makes a spinning toy slow down?

When forces act on a moving spinning toy they can make it slow down. One force that can make a spinning toy slow down is **friction**.

The force of friction makes this toy rocket ride slow down.

Friction is a force between two surfaces that are touching one another. With a spinning toy, there can be friction between different parts of the toy. Friction acts in the opposite direction to the toy's movement.

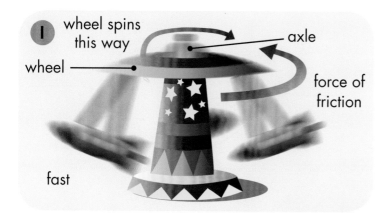

Friction between this toy rocket ride's **wheel** and **axle** makes it slow down.

What makes a spinning toy stop moving?

When forces act on a spinning toy they can make it slow down and stop moving. One force that can make a spinning toy stop moving is **friction**.

The force of friction will eventually make this spinning top stop moving.

With a spinning toy, there is friction between the toy and the ground. Friction makes spinning toys slow down and eventually stop moving.

1

top spins quickly

force of friction

The force of friction between this spinning top and the floor will make the top stop spinning.

2

top spins slowly

force of friction

3

top stops moving

What else affects how a spinning toy moves?

Something else that affects how a spinning toy moves is how heavy it is. This affects the amount of force needed to change how the toy moves.

How heavy a merry-go-round is affects how easy it is to move it using a pushing force.

The heavier a spinning toy is, the larger the force that is needed to change the way it moves. A heavier toy needs a larger pushing force to make it spin.

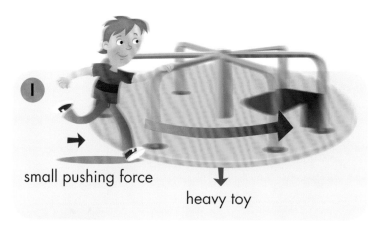

small pushing force

heavy toy

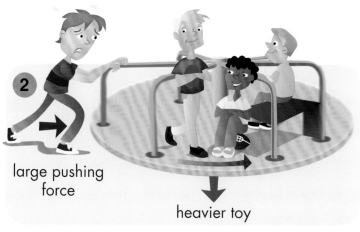

large pushing force

heavier toy

You need to apply a larger pushing force to move a heavier merry-go-round.

Make a spinning toy: Paper windmill

This paper windmill is easy to make and fun to play with.

Ask a carer or teacher for help.

What you need:

- 1 A4 sheet of pale-coloured lightweight card
- coloured pencils
- scissors
- drawing pin
- a bead
- thin wooden rod (about 30 centimetres long).

The force created by moving air makes this paper windmill spin.

What to do:

1 Decorate both sides of the card using the coloured pencils.

2 Fold the card so that the bottom edge lines up with the side edge.

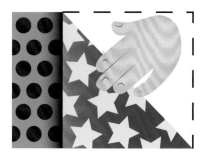

3 Cut off the extra card.

4 Fold the card in half from corner to corner, then unfold the card.

5 Make a pencil mark on each of the fold lines, halfway from the centre.

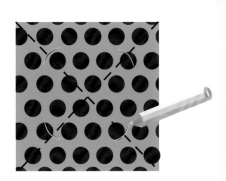

6 Cut along the fold lines. Stop at the pencil marks.

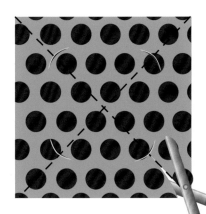

7 Bring every second point into the centre.

8 Stick a drawing pin through all four points from the front.

9 Put a bead on the end of the drawing pin and then stick the pin into the wooden rod.

bead

10 Your paper windmill is ready to spin!

Experiment: Can hot water make a spinning toy spin?

Try this experiment to find out whether hot water can make a spinning toy spin.

What you need:
- cold water
- saucepan
- cooktop
- oven glove
- paper windmill.

Never use a stove without an adult. Ask a carer or teacher for help.

What to do:

1 Fill a saucepan halfway with cold water.

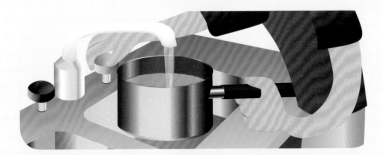

2 Put on the oven glove and place the saucepan on the cooktop.

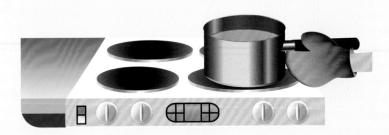

3 Turn the stove on to a high heat.

4 Keep an eye on the water as it heats up.

5 When the water is boiling, put on the oven glove and hold half of the paper windmill above the saucepan. What happens?

What happens?

The paper windmill should start spinning when you hold it above the saucepan.

Why does it happen?

When water is heated, some of it turns into **steam**. Steam rises. The rising steam applies a pushing force to the arms of the paper windmill. This pushing force makes the paper windmill start spinning.

windmill spins

pushing force of rising steam

The pushing force of rising steam makes the paper windmill start spinning.

How forces make spinning toys work

This table shows some of the pushing and pulling forces that act on spinning toys.

Forces make toys ...	Pushing or pulling force?	Example of the force acting on a toy	
start moving	pushing force	A yoyo starts moving when a pushing force acts on it, together with the pushing force of **gravity**.	
change direction	pushing force	A windmill changes direction when the pushing force created by moving air acts on it.	
speed up	pushing force	A moving totem tennis ball speeds up when a larger pushing force acts on it.	
slow down	pushing force	A toy rocket ride slows down when the pushing force of **friction** acts on it.	
stop moving	pushing force	A spinning top stops moving when the pushing force of friction acts on it.	

Glossary

axis
the imaginary line around which a spinning object spins

axle
a rod that passes through the middle of a wheel and works by holding the wheel in place and allowing it to turn

friction
a force that slows down moving objects, and acts in the opposite direction to the direction the object is moving in

gravity
the force that pulls objects towards Earth, and acts on everything, all the time

steam
the gas that boiling water turns into

wheel
a round disc with an axle through the middle, which works by turning around the axle

Index